GW00375168

50 TIPS

TO HELP YOU DEAL WITH

ANXIETY

50 TIPS TO HELP YOU DEAL WITH ANXIETY

Copyright © Summersdale Publishers Ltd, 2014

With research by Emily Kearns

All rights reserved.

No part of this book may be reproduced by any means, nor transmitted, nor translated into a machine language, without the written permission of the publishers.

Condition of Sale
This book is sold subject to the condition that it shall not, by way of trade or otherwise, be lent, re-sold, hired out or otherwise circulated in any form of binding or cover other than that in which it is published and without a similar condition including this condition being imposed on the subsequent purchaser.

Vie Books is an imprint of Summersdale Publishers Ltd

Summersdale Publishers Ltd
46 West Street
Chichester
West Sussex
PO19 1RP
UK

www.summersdale.com

Printed and bound in the Czech Republic

ISBN: 978-1-84953-580-9

Substantial discounts on bulk quantities of Summersdale books are available to corporations, professional associations and other organisations. For details contact Nicky Douglas by telephone: +44 (0) 1243 756902, fax: +44 (0) 1243 786300, or email: nicky@summersdale.com.

50 TIPS

TO HELP YOU DEAL WITH

ANXIETY

Anna Barnes

Introduction

It is rare for a person to go through life without feeling anxious from time to time. Some of us are better equipped than others to deal with life's daily struggles; some of us suffer greater struggles than others. The way we deal with our anxieties is key to our general wellbeing, and there are plenty of changes we can make to help us take a more positive outlook and feel calmer in certain situations. The suggestions here may not make you feel different overnight, but this book offers tips to help you improve your mood, diet and health, and hopefully get you on the right path so that you can tackle your demons with a renewed, positive attitude.

SECTION ONE:

IDENTIFYING ANXIETY

In order to help lessen feelings of anxiety, first
we need to understand where they come from.
These tips will help you to spot the symptoms
and causes of anxiety.

Understand anxiety

Anxiety can manifest as a feeling of unease, nervousness or concern, often with regard to a particular situation or predicament. Suffering from anxiety is not abnormal; it's unusual not to feel anxious every now and again, but when you can no longer shake these feelings and they begin to overwhelm you, then you may need to take steps to get help or adjust aspects of your daily life to improve your situation. Feeling tense when faced with a daunting situation – perhaps an exam, a job interview or a driving test – is perfectly natural, but when tension builds to a point where you find it difficult to function normally, it could be time to take action.

2

Spot the symptoms

Do you feel unusually tense most of the time? Perhaps you find yourself overthinking the finer details of every situation, or you have irrational fears that seem to follow you around. When feeling nervous or under pressure, you might feel your heart pounding in your chest and your breathing quicken. Experts have identified this as the 'fight or flight' reflex, which is our bodies' natural response to stressful situations. Anxiety causes your body to release adrenaline, which makes your heart beat faster and breathing become more rapid; it is the body's way of preparing to defend itself from a potentially dangerous situation. However, if you don't use the adrenaline, by fighting or running, then it takes longer for it to subside and may leave you feeling agitated.

Learn why it affects you

Some people suffer from bouts of anxiety linked to distressing past experiences – and the thought of having to deal with a similar experience again makes them feel tense and apprehensive. Others may experience anxiety brought on by poor diet, lack of exercise, drug misuse, exhaustion or stress. Some anxiety sufferers worry excessively about the future and feel they are not in control of their own lives, while others harbour major concerns about things beyond their control, such as developing a serious illness, losing their job, or even global warming and world hunger. Use the tips in this book to help you to find positivity and a place in your mind where you feel comfortable to relax. Just a few small changes can make a difference.

4

Keep a diary

It's important to identify what triggers your anxiety, and keeping a note of when it occurs can really help. Write regularly in a dedicated anxiety diary, and keep track of your feelings and emotions in this way. By keeping a record of any bouts of anxiety you will be able to spot patterns in your behaviour and identify the cause of any attacks. You may also find it useful to mark each occurrence of anxiety out of ten, in order to assess the severity of different situations. You can then take steps to work on changing how you respond to these situations and in turn feel better about yourself.

COPING DAY
TO DAY

Learning to cope with anxiety on a day-to-day basis is the first step. Using these helpful suggestions to change little things could make a big difference to your daily wellbeing.

5

Identify your triggers

Everyone is different and each of us have anxieties that are brought on by different situations and for any number of reasons. In order to help improve our outlook, it's important to identify the areas of our lives in which we feel the most anxiety. Whether you feel anxious about driving your car in rush hour or coping with mounting bills, there are ways you can tackle these situations head on.

Instead of driving during rush hour, try public transport; to prevent the bills mounting, create a spreadsheet detailing your monthly outgoings, so you can keep track of them in a clear and manageable fashion. Look for signs of what causes your anxiety so you can find remedies.

Be prepared

If you anticipate an event or situation that is likely to make you feel anxious, do your best to prepare for it. This might sound like common sense, but when feeling anxious we sometimes forget to approach things logically. If you have to take a test or an exam, draw up a revision timetable in advance so you can cover all the ground required. If you feel anxious about giving a presentation at work, spend plenty of time preparing and perhaps ask a colleague to present with you. If you're a nervous driver and the thought of having to use the car makes you feel anxious, try a driving refresher course. Being prepared for a situation will help you to relax.

Overcome stress at work

Are you finding work stressful? You're not alone. More and more people are finding themselves overworked and underpaid, as many businesses struggle to compete and are forced to lay off staff. There's still just as much work to do, but fewer people to do it. If your job is starting to make you feel anxious all the time, even when you're at home, perhaps you should talk to someone. If your line manager or boss is not the approachable sort, how about telling a colleague and see if they're feeling the same way. If you are still concerned, you could talk to someone in the HR department; this is your health and wellbeing after all.

Improve your work environment

No matter how many times you tell yourself it's just a job, it's likely that you spend more time in the workplace than you do awake in your own home during a working week. If your job leads you to have regular bouts of anxiety – perhaps it's a high-pressure position, or you have a particularly demanding boss or colleagues – there are steps you can take to help improve your situation. If you find your workload is simply too much, think about delegating tasks to others who might not have as much on their plates. Learn how to manage your time effectively, and create a timetable if you feel this helps. Keeping a diary of the time spent on each task in a working day could be useful if you ever find you simply can't cope with what's being asked of you and need to talk to a manager about it. It's also important to learn how to say 'no' – there are only so many hours in the day and if you don't have time to do something, someone else will have to. Make your work environment a nicer place to be: add a plant or a photograph to your area and declutter for a sense of calm. You should also make sure you take regular breaks.

Tackle money matters

If your finances are causing you to experience anxiety, the first thing to do is get organised and create a spreadsheet detailing all your monthly outgoings. Then, work out where you might be able to cut back. Do you have the best possible energy tariff, for example? There are several price-comparison websites that could help you switch to a more cost-efficient price plan. What about your mobile phone: are you paying for 'free' minutes that you don't actually use? It might be time to downgrade or switch to pay-as-you-go or a SIM-only deal. How much food do you throw away each week/month? Make shopping lists and stick to them, freeze any leftovers to eat at a later date and use a price-comparison site such as www.mysupermarket.co.uk to make sure you're shopping sensibly.

Learn to manage your thoughts

It's important to learn how to switch off – don't let anxiety follow you around all day. When at work, focus on the task at hand and try not to let your mind wander to other aspects of your life that may be causing you to feel tense. If a stressful work environment is getting you down out of hours, try to leave all negative thoughts about your job in the workplace when you clock out for the day. If you find it difficult to switch off in the evenings, make plans to take your mind off work – see friends, go to the cinema or sign up for that evening class you've always been meaning to take.

Enjoy a treat a day

If you're feeling low, tense or anxious, try doing something nice, however small, each day to lift your spirits. Whether it's putting fresh sheets on the bed, making time to watch your favourite film or TV programme, disappearing under a blanket to read a book, cooking a nice meal or seeing a friend, having something to look forward to throughout the day will help you through and raise your positivity levels. Look at your diary regularly and make sure you have enough going on each week to keep you occupied and happy. And you don't have to spend money to have fun: on a sunny evening go for a walk around the local park; when it's cold, head to a friend's house or investigate the free events in your local area.

12

Know your goals

Do you know what you want from life? Are you happy in your work? What about your home and personal life? If your current life situation is causing you to suffer from anxiety, it could be time to make some changes. Think about your job, your relationships, your finances and your friendships. What could you change that might make you feel more positive going forward? Set realistic goals that help you to feel inspired to make changes – and choose the goals that are right for you, not to please anyone else. Try writing down your aspirations and, if it suits, create a realistic plan detailing when you hope to have achieved them. If it's a career change that you crave, why not do some research and seek professional career advice? Tell yourself that by this time next year you will be on the path to making a change in that area of your life.

13

Try something new

Positive change could be what you need if you want to improve your current situation, so why not try something new? Get involved in a new hobby or activity. Whether it's joining a gym, trying a yoga, Pilates or martial arts course, learning another language or the basics of photography at the local college, or crocheting an enormous blanket, it could be a good idea to have a project to get your teeth into, to give you focus and take your mind off your anxiety. Evening classes and courses are also a good way to meet new people – and don't let this worry you, everyone is in the same boat so relax and enjoy it.

BOOST
YOUR MOOD

Try these proven mood boosters for a more positive outlook and you could be on the path to a happier, healthier you.

Learn to de-stress

When feeling anxious, the last thing you need is unnecessary stress throughout your daily life. Try taking things one step at a time and don't take too much on – either at work or in your personal life. Perhaps you have small children or an ageing parent to care for – don't be afraid to ask friends and family for help if things get too much; and work regular hours to gain a sense of day-to-day consistency. It's important to slow down if daily life is getting on top of you – make lists and cross off tasks when you complete them to feel a sense of achievement. And don't forget that sometimes you might just need to close a door on everything and have a good cry. Allowing your emotions to surface can have a positive impact, and is likely to leave you feeling somewhat relieved and ready to face the world again.

15

Beat the blues

Experts have found that anxiety and depression often go hand in hand, and when in the grips of depression it can be difficult to see the light at the end of the tunnel. If these simple steps to providing a better, healthier and more positive life for yourself don't seem to be shaking the blues, you may need to seek help from a professional. Check out the support services in your local area and, if all else fails, see a doctor. They will be able to provide you with information and helpful suggestions to get you back on track and feeling yourself again.

16

Join a support group

Don't feel that you are alone in suffering from anxiety; the Mental Health Foundation estimates that one in four people in the UK will experience a mental health issue over the course of a year, and claims anxiety and depression are the most common mental health disorders in the country. Mind, the mental health charity, offers help and advice, either over the phone or via its website www.mind.org.uk, and has centres located in major towns and cities offering crisis helplines, supported housing and counselling. Search for support groups in your local area and spend some time with people experiencing similar difficulties – it will be just as beneficial for them as it will be for you.

17

Talk about it

One of the best things you can do when trying to understand your anxiety, and where it comes from, is to talk to a friend or family member. Vocalising your concerns is not only cathartic, but may help you to understand why you feel the way you do; and if you speak to someone who knows you well, they may be able to offer valuable insight into how they perceive your recent behaviour. You're also likely to feel a sense of relief after speaking to someone whom you trust, so give it a go and confide in someone close to you.

Think positively

Although it's often easier said than done, it's important to make an effort to stay as positive as possible if you're prone to bouts of anxiety. Believe in your ability to change and try to see the good in situations that have caused you anxiety in the past. Why not do someone a good turn and see how their appreciation lifts your mood? This will not only help to take your mind off your symptoms, but is likely to improve your outlook in the long run. Keep active and busy, focus on your work, and regularly meet with family and friends. Talk to others who share similar symptoms and share tips on how to stay on top of things. Keeping those negative thoughts at bay will have a positive impact on your anxiety as a whole.

Try laughter therapy

When we laugh, our muscles relax and endorphins (the body's natural painkillers) are released into the bloodstream. Stand in an empty room and force yourself to laugh – you feel silly, don't you? It might sound unusual, but it really works. Take things one step further and get some friends together for a laughter therapy session. Sit in a circle and take it in turns to start. The first person should say 'ha', the second 'ha ha', the third 'ha ha ha' and so on until everyone dissolves into laughter. You can also try this lying on the floor with your heads resting on each other's stomachs – potentially funnier and likely to result in more giggling.

Get out in the sun

We might be prone to drizzly, grey days in the UK, but when the sun does come out it's important to take advantage of it. Our bodies create most of our vitamin D from direct sunlight and this in turn helps our brains to produce serotonin, the 'happy hormone'. Fewer hours of sunlight in the winter months can lead us to feel sleepier than usual, as when it is dark our brains produce melatonin, the 'sleep hormone', which may make us feel drowsier than usual. Evidence suggests that short, daily periods of direct sunlight – just ten to 15 minutes – can provide the vitamin D we need to see us through; after this you should apply sun cream to avoid sun damage.

TURN TO EXERCISE

Exercise benefits your brain as well as your body and it doesn't have to be gruelling. See how you can incorporate light activity into your daily routine to help relieve stress.

Get active

With more of us than ever working in office jobs, it's easy to let the week go by without seeing much in the way of daylight or doing much physical activity other than walking to and from the car, train station or bus stop. During exercise, the body releases serotonin, the 'happy hormone', which is both a mood booster and stress buster. Being more active will help you to relax in your downtime, sleep better and increase positivity, all of which will ultimately help ease anxiety. If you're struggling to fit in exercise, why not get off the bus a few stops earlier and walk the rest of the way? Or leave the car at home if you only need to make a short trip.

22

Swim for it

Swimming is a great form of exercise that offers positive health benefits – both physically and psychologically. As well as helping to tone and strengthen muscles, increase your flexibility and help keep your heart healthy, spending half an hour in the pool can instil a sense of calm and help you to feel more in control. When swimming, you need to concentrate on your movements and breathing, thus bringing your focus to the activity at hand and away from any anxieties you may be feeling. Give your local swimming pool a go and, if it works for you, think about signing up for a membership so you will be inclined to go for a dip more often.

Get on your bike

As well as an efficient mode of transport, cycling is the perfect way to fit exercise into your daily routine. If you currently drive to work, or use public transport, and the distance is manageable, think about dusting off your steed and cycling to work instead. Fresh air and exercise are a good combination to help raise positivity levels, and regular cycling could go a long way to assist in easing your anxiety. If you'd rather take the scenic route, visit the Sustrans website, www.sustrans.org.uk, and learn about the cycling routes in your area.

The UK National Cycle Network comprises 14,000 miles of safe, traffic-free paths and quiet road routes throughout the country, and Sustrans claims that a safe NCN route passes within a mile of 55 per cent of all UK homes. There's a wealth of green space on the outskirts of your home town just waiting to be explored, so get on your bike and ride your way to a more positive outlook.

24

Get walking

If cycling doesn't appeal, you can still get outside and transport yourself from place to place on two legs – another great way to get fresh air and sunshine, while boosting your mood and general fitness levels. If you don't live close to any pleasant, green spaces, make a conscious effort to walk rather than drive or use public transport, where possible; walking around a city can really open your eyes to things you might not have noticed before. Alternatively, you could go on a day trip to a nearby green space and take in a loop walk or plan a weekend away to a national park — this will not only give you something to look forward to, but will no doubt offer a sense of achievement once you've hiked to the top of a great big hill and surveyed the surrounding scenery. Visit www.nationaltrail.co.uk or www.nationaltrust.org.uk to find suitable walking routes in your area.

DE-STRESS
YOUR DIET

Experts have found a number of links between diet and mental health. Follow these tips to see how you can equip your mind to keep anxiety at bay by eating the right foods.

Eat regularly

When assessing your diet and how you might be able to change it to improve your mood, the most important factor is the regularity of your meals. It's important to eat three meals a day at regularly spaced intervals in order to maintain blood sugar levels. Breakfast really is the most important meal of the day – if you skip this you will experience a dip in blood sugar and this can lead to low mood. If you start to feel hungry and irritable in between meals, reach for a healthy snack, such as a banana or a handful of nuts.

Pep up with protein

It's important to eat enough protein, particularly when suffering from a bout of anxiety. Protein helps your brain to absorb tryptophan, which is the amino acid needed for the production of serotonin. Tryptophan- and protein-rich foods include chicken, lamb, fish, soya beans and many nuts and seeds. Walnuts, flaxseeds, pumpkin and sunflower seeds are a particularly good source of tryptophan; sprinkle them on salads or, if you're not a big fan, use a coffee grinder to reduce them to a fine powder and add the mixture to soups and stews. You won't even know it's there, but will be reaping the benefits. Tryptophan-rich foods could well help you sleep better and elevate your mood too.

Focus on healthy fats

Not all fats are bad news. We all need to consume enough healthy fats to keep our brains functioning properly, and research has found that those who diet and cut out all types of fat can suffer from symptoms of anxiety and depression. Of the four types of fat, the unhealthy varieties, saturated (found in certain meats and dairy products, and, to a lesser degree, eggs) and trans fats (mainly found in fried and baked foods), should be avoided or consumed in moderation. However, polyunsaturated fats are vital in maintaining a healthy brain, while monounsaturated fats are rich in vitamin E, and both can help to lower cholesterol. The former can be found in walnuts, peanuts, sesame and sunflower seeds, olive oil and oily fish; while the latter can be found in nuts, olives and avocados.

Va va those vitamins

In the UK, the recommended daily intake of fruit and vegetables is five portions a day. The fruit and vegetables you need the most are those containing B vitamins and vitamin C – all linked to healthy brain function – as these will help your body to control your anxiety and boost your mood. Find B vitamins in green leafy vegetables, beetroot, mushrooms and citrus fruits; and find vitamin C in oranges, red and green peppers, broccoli, strawberries, blackcurrants, Brussels sprouts and potatoes. It's also important to keep up levels of vitamins D and E, which are both found to support better mental function: find vitamin D in oily fish, such as salmon, mackerel and sardines, eggs and fortified breakfast cereals; and find vitamin E in nuts, seeds and fortified cereals.

29

Max your minerals

Minerals are essential for a healthy nervous system, so to ensure general physical and mental wellbeing, you need to consume the correct amounts. Calcium deficiency has been linked to irritability, nervousness and an inability to relax; find calcium in dairy foods such as cheese, yoghurt and milk. Magnesium is often referred to as 'nature's tranquiliser' and plays an essential role in helping the body absorb calcium; you can find it in dark-green, leafy vegetables (such as broccoli, kale and spinach), seafood, potatoes, nuts, seeds and wholegrain products. A lack of zinc has been linked to depression; find zinc in seafood, eggs, broccoli, mushrooms, nuts, seeds and kiwis. Depleted iron levels in your diet can lead to low mood and anxiety, so it's important to ensure that you eat sufficient iron to meet your needs. Women need to keep an eye on their iron levels, as they tend to need more than men, and vegetarians might want to think about taking a supplement; find iron in dark-green, leafy vegetables, meat, fish, beans, pulses, nuts and wholegrain products.

Try supplements

There are several herbal supplements that could help you banish anxiety. Valerian, hops and passion flower have all been found to relieve stress and anxiety, as well as promote healthy sleep; and while rhodiola rosea has been found to help with mild anxiety, it is also said to boost concentration. St John's Wort is used to treat mild to moderate depression and has been found to assist in easing anxiety, but if you decide to try taking it, consult a doctor or pharmacist as it can react with several common prescription medicines, including the contraceptive pill.

Stay hydrated

Dehydration won't bring on a bout of anxiety on its own, but if you are already suffering from stress and tension, it may well aggravate your condition. If you are prone to panic attacks, it's especially important to stay hydrated as this will lessen the chances of you experiencing common symptoms, which could trigger an attack, such as headaches, feeling light-headed, muscle weakness and an increased heart rate. The European Food Safety Authority recommends 1.6 litres of fluid a day for women and 2 litres for men, so try to get used to carrying a bottle of water around with you, and take frequent drinks to stay hydrated. Don't forget that hot drinks, fruit juices and food also contain water, and so count towards your recommended daily intake.

Cut down on caffeine and alcohol

When suffering from the physical symptoms of anxiety, it might be an idea to cut down on tea or coffee. Caffeine is a stimulant, which increases mental and physical functioning, and therefore will increase any anxiety that you may be feeling. Alcohol, on the other hand, is a depressant, which tends to alter or exaggerate your current state of mind. So, if you're feeling tense and anxious, instead of helping you to relax there's a chance that your favourite tipple could have the opposite effect and aggravate your symptoms.

Give green tea a go

If you're trying to cut down on caffeine, consider replacing some of your daily cups of tea or coffee with green tea. Green tea contains much lower levels of caffeine and the amino acid L-theanine, which has been found to have calming effects, and many claim it's a good anti-anxiety remedy. If you don't like the taste of straight green tea, why not try one of the many variants on the market? Green teas are available in a multitude of flavours, including strawberry, mandarin, echinacea (good for warding off colds), mint, ginseng (for that all-important pick-me-up you won't be getting from your caffeine fix) and nettle.

SECTION SIX:

SLEEP WELL

Everyone is different when it comes to how much sleep they need, but if you suffer from anxiety it's important not to cause any unnecessary stress through tiredness.

34

Make your bedroom enticing

The optimum amount of sleep for most adults is between seven and nine hours a night – work out yours and try to stick to it. Make your bedroom your sanctuary – a place for sleep and sex only. Leave your worries in another room and switch off while you prepare for sleep. One of the best ways to promote restful sleep is to declutter your surroundings. Keep your bedroom tidy, with floors clear, and find a home somewhere else in the house for everything that doesn't naturally belong there. Remove any tablets, phones, laptops and televisions – screen time should be limited before bedtime to prevent your brain 'waking up' when it's really time to go to sleep. Read a book or a magazine instead. Opt for soft lighting to give the room a warm glow, and try scented candles or oils to further create a relaxing and pleasant atmosphere. Lavender, chamomile, jasmine and vanilla are all believed to promote restful sleep.

35

Learn to clear your mind

One of the most common causes of sleep loss is an overburdened mind. We've all experienced it, some more than others. It's important to learn to pack up your worries before you head to bed. You might find that writing down how you're feeling will help to unburden you – perhaps you could write in a diary or make a to-do list for the next day. You might also find that talking to a friend or family member helps to ease your anxiety; the aim is to feel as stress-free as possible before your head hits the pillow. Have a bath using some essential oils, but nothing too overpowering, to help you wind down, and drink a cup of herbal tea. If possible, choose one featuring lavender, chamomile, vanilla, hops and valerian. If you're still struggling to get to sleep, you could try something a little stronger, such as valerian root tablets, which are widely available, or a pillow spray designed to help you sleep.

Control the temperature

If you feel too hot or too cold, this is likely to inhibit restful sleep. Know your own body temperature and prepare your bedroom for sleep accordingly. Come summer, do you find yourself flinging off the duvet in the middle of the night? If so, why not opt for cotton sheets instead or a thinner duvet more suited to the season; leave the window open or set up a fan to allow cool airflow through the bedroom. If you bury yourself under the duvet and lie there shivering in the winter, you may find an electric blanket, hot water bottle, or thermal or fleecy pyjamas do the trick.

Switch off screens

Research has found that too much time in front of backlit devices, such as televisions, computers or laptops, tablets or mobile phones, can have a detrimental effect on our ability to get to sleep. Two or more hours of exposure to any of the above devices has been found to suppress melatonin, the sleep hormone, which in turn can hinder sleep. If you can take a break from any screens before bedtime then you are likely to reap the sleep-laden benefits, but if you absolutely have to check your emails, at least dim the brightness on your device and don't spend too long lingering over the screen. Remove all devices from your bedroom and try using a good old-fashioned alarm clock instead of your phone to avoid the temptation to tweet, text or email just before bed.

Get the bed right

It's likely that you spend seven to nine hours a night in your bed – and possibly more at weekends – so it's important to choose one that's right for you. There are several things to think about. Is the bed the right size? If you share it with a partner, do you find their movement throughout the night disturbs you? Perhaps you need a bigger bed. If you wake up complaining of aches and pains, you may well find your mattress isn't the right fit for you. With so many choices available today, you can afford to be picky. Rather than ordering anything online, go into a mattress showroom and test out the beds. Everyone does it so don't be embarrassed. If you find you can't afford your dream model, perhaps a mattress topper will help.

39

Devise a bedtime routine

If you find your anxiety is causing you to feel tense at bedtime and not ready for restful sleep, try devising a bedtime routine. If you stick to it, a routine around the time you'd like to go to bed will help to let your body know that it's time to go to sleep and prepare accordingly. Perhaps you could have a bath, followed by a hot drink while you read a book. Eventually, these regular pre-bedtime activities will act as triggers and tell your body and mind to switch off and go to sleep.

TAKE TIME OUT

If you feel things are just getting too much, it's important to take time out and relax. Follow these tips to help you to become more mindful, and gain a sense of calm and perspective.

Make time for yourself

If you have other people in your life to worry about and you find this adds to your anxieties, then be sure to set aside time just for you. When there's a lot going on, it's important to have time to yourself to relax and gather your thoughts. Whether you spend an evening curled up with a good book or your favourite film or take yourself off for a scenic walk, find the time to do something you enjoy and appreciate your own company. Going for a run or a swim will give you a chance to think about your day, while doing something that will have a positive effect on your body and mind.

Take time off

Whatever your job, it's vital that you take regular breaks from work and spend time doing what makes you happy. Whether you go on holiday or stay at home, you need time away from your daily work routine to relax and switch off, and just forget about it all for a few days or a week. The 'staycation' has become ever more popular, while many people take time off to get things done that they wouldn't usually have time for – such as odd jobs around the house or catching up with friends.

Try a spa day

A real treat to send you to new heights of relaxation is to book a spa day or weekend, where there is little to do but swim, sit in a sauna or hot tub, and enjoy blissful treatments, such as an aromatherapy massage or a facial. This needn't be expensive – there are plenty of websites offering discounted spa experiences, and it's likely you'll be able to find one not too far away. Keep an eye on www.groupon.com, www.livingsocial.com, www.lastminute.com and www.spabreaks.com for special offers, and arrange to get away from it all for a day or two.

Practise Pilates

Pilates is a low-impact, mindful form of exercise designed to strengthen the abdominal muscles, while promoting good posture, and lengthening and strengthening all the muscles in the body. Devised by German gymnast and bodybuilder Joseph Pilates in the early twentieth century, Pilates has grown increasingly in popularity in recent years and been found to have a positive effect on mood and anxiety through its encouragement of deep, controlled breathing. Visit www.pilatesfoundation.com to learn more and to find a teacher in your local area. If there isn't a teacher nearby, you could buy a DVD and learn from that, or try watching some videos on YouTube.

44

Give yoga a go

Yoga can be practised in several different forms, but the ideal type to ease anxiety and tension is hatha. Hatha yoga is a gentle form of exercise that involves moving the body into, and holding, various postures, while maintaining slow, regular breathing. Designed to improve posture, strengthen muscles and increase flexibility, yoga also aims to help clear your mind and instil a sense of calm, and has been found to greatly help with alleviating stress and anxiety. You're likely to find several yoga options available locally, but start with something fairly gentle and meditative. If you can't find a hatha class or would rather try it out on your own first, buy one of the many DVDs available and practise in the comfort of your own home.

45

Make time for meditation and mindfulness

Studies have found that meditation can have a profound effect on those suffering from severe anxiety. Meditation is a mental discipline in which you train your mind to focus and be still. The idea is to exist in the moment and clear all thoughts and worries from your mind, which can be helpful in easing anxiety and stress. The practice of mindfulness – which teaches us to live in the moment in all aspects of our lives – has also been found to help anxiety sufferers who tend to focus on past events or anticipate those in the future. The ability to train your mind to be aware of your feelings in certain situations can help you to identify your anxiety triggers and equip you to better deal with your attacks.

Embrace essential oils and massage

Massage can help to relieve any physical tension you might be feeling and will have a calming effect on your mind too. You could opt for a professional massage or ask your partner to help. There is a range of essential oils that are thought to have a calming influence, so use one of these to enhance the benefits of the massage. Alternatively, you could dab a little onto your wrists or behind your ears, so the scent stays with you, and this may help you to relax throughout your day. Bergamot and jasmine are known for their calming and uplifting capabilities, while lemon balm and lavender are thought to help relieve stress and anxiety.

EXPLORE THE BENEFITS OF TREATMENT

When the world gets on top of you, you might feel you want to escape. Try these techniques to ease your anxiety and feel emotionally and physically lighter.

47

Seek cognitive behavioural therapy

Cognitive behavioural therapy (CBT) is a form of psychotherapy that helps you to focus on replacing negative thoughts and behaviour with a more positive outlook. Your negative thoughts and behaviour affect your feelings, and this is what leads you to feel anxious. Cognitive theory claims our negative thoughts come from experiences throughout childhood and early adulthood, which often stay with us as we go through life. It works on the principles that you can change these perceptions of negativity by focusing on the present, with practical ways to improve your outlook on a daily basis, thus eventually altering the way you think and behave. The Mind website, www.mind.org.uk, is a good source of information and will help you to locate a therapist in your area.

48

Discover homeopathy

Homeopathy is a form of complementary medicine used to treat a wide range of conditions on the basis that 'like cures like' – meaning a substance taken in minimal amounts will help to cure the condition it would cause if it were administered in larger amounts. Homeopathic medicines are made largely from plants and minerals and are available over the counter, but you'd be advised to see a homeopath to learn what approach would be best for your symptoms. Visit www.britishhomeopathic.org to learn more about the practice, to find a homeopath in your area, and to learn about both the private and NHS treatments available.

Heal with hypnosis

Many anxiety sufferers have found that hypnosis can help them to remain calm and keep control while experiencing panic attacks, and there are CDs and downloadable MP3s that can guide you. Basic self-hypnosis is something you can learn and use when you feel the onset of such an attack. The key is to remain as calm as possible and take yourself to a space where you can be alone or at least feel comfortable. Focus on your breathing – keeping it steady, deep and slow – then close your eyes and imagine yourself walking down a long set of steps in a place that makes you feel safe, perhaps a beautiful garden. From the crown of your head to your toes, begin to relax each part of your body, bit by bit, all the while walking further down the steps in your mind. Once you've done that, you need to repeat a positive statement to yourself — something like, 'I am relaxed, I am confident, I can do this.' When you start to feel calm, imagine yourself walking slowly back up those steps, all the while repeating your positive statement. When you reach the top, take a deep breath and open your eyes.

Talk to a doctor

If you've given everything else a try and your anxiety is still proving too much for you, it could be time to seek professional help. Go to your GP first and see what they suggest – they may recommend seeing a therapist, someone you can talk to about your anxieties; or cognitive behavioural therapy; or even medication. Remember to be honest with your doctor – try not to hold back, and give as much detail as possible – and they'll be able to suggest the right solution for you and your anxieties. Complementary therapies can help a great deal to reduce the stresses and strains that could be causing you to experience bouts of anxiety but, sometimes, professional help is what's needed. You'll be on the right track and in safe hands, and will feel the benefit before you know it.

Notes

50 TIPS
TO HELP YOU
DE-STRESS

Anna Barnes

50 TIPS TO HELP YOU DE-STRESS

Anna Barnes

ISBN: 978-1-84953-402-4

Hardback

£5.99

No matter how hard we try, there are times for all of us when the stresses and strains of daily life start to pile up. This book of simple, easy-to-follow tips gives you the tools and techniques you need to recognise your stress triggers and learn to take life as it comes, with a calm and balanced outlook.

50 TIPS
TO BUILD YOUR
SELF-ESTEEM

Anna Barnes

50 TIPS TO BUILD YOUR SELF-ESTEEM

Anna Barnes

ISBN: 978-1-84953-509-0

Hardback

£5.99

Having a healthy, positive sense of self-esteem enables us to avoid the obstacles that can hold us back and to really make the most of life, even when we face knockbacks.

This book of simple, easy-to-follow tips provides you with the tools and techniques needed to feel better inside and out, making you a more confident and positive person.

If you're interested in finding out more about our books,
find us on Facebook at **Summersdale Publishers**
and follow us on Twitter at **@Summersdale**.

www.summersdale.com